Transportation

Written by Rozanne Lanczak Williams

Editor: Susan R. Friedman

Illustrator: Catherine Yuh

Project Director: Carolea Williams

Table of Contents

Introduction 3

Getting Started
Classroom Environment 4
Things That Go (reproducible) 6
Auto Body Shop (reproducible) 7
Management ◆ Assessment 8
Performance Evaluation (reproducible) 9
Parent Letter (reproducible) 10

**Reading &
Language Arts**
Peek-a-Boo Plane ◆ Transportation Poetry 11
Peek-a-Boo Plane (reproducible) 12
Journeys through Writing 13
Bus Pattern (reproducible) 14

Mathematics
All Aboard the Number Train 15
Number Train (reproducibles) 16
Ordinal Numbers 18
Who Came in First? (reproducible) 19

Science
Transportation Study ◆ Will It Float like a Boat? . . . 20
Gravity and Transportation 21

**Social Studies &
Geography**
Map Skills ◆ Staying Safe with Seat Belts ◆
    Community-Helper Vehicles 22
Community-Helper Vehicles (reproducible) 23

Music & Drama
Flying High ◆ Favorite Transportation Songs 24
Pilot's Hat (reproducible) 25

Physical Education
Safari Tour ◆ Train Relay Game 26

Arts & Crafts
Constructing Crazy Cars ◆ Safety Signs 27
Milk-Carton Steamships ◆ Cool Cardboard Cars . . . 28

Cooking
Banana Boats ◆ Celery Carts 29

Special Events
Field Trips ◆ Transportation Experts 30

Student Awards 31

Recommended Books 32

Introduction

Use thematic teaching in the classroom and watch your students thrive in a cooperative, creative learning environment that emphasizes thinking, speaking, reading, and writing. CTP's *Primary Theme Series* helps you organize your time, materials, and classroom space while providing fun, thought-provoking activities that all students will enjoy.

The *Transportation* book takes students on a tour of transportation. Students explore, investigate, analyze, and discuss topics such as

- types of transportation.
- uses of transportation.
- ways transportation is helpful to the community.
- how gravity affects transportation.
- safety and transportation.

Hands-on, integrated activities include

- making "things that go" wind socks.
- observing how gravity affects transportation.
- building "peek-a-boo" planes.
- examining different kinds of maps.
- reading and dramatizing favorite transportation poems and songs.

The *Transportation* book also provides several reproducible sheets, including a performance-evaluation form, a parent letter, and student certificates. Introduce your students to a world of adventure, curiosity, and fun by teaching them all about transportation.

 # Getting Started

Classroom Environment

Create a learning center in a corner of the classroom for students to use throughout the unit. Display pictures of various types of transportation, and set up an inviting reading area that includes a class library of transportation books (see Recommended Books, page 32). Invite students to bring their favorite transportation models or toys to display in a special section of the learning center. For extra motivation, use airplane and bus cutouts to mark the days on the class calendar, to keep track of skills mastered, and to reward students for good performance.

◆ ◆ ◆ ◆ ◆ ◆ ◆ ◆ ◆ ◆ ◆ ◆ ◆

On the Go Wall Mural

Invite the class to create a wall mural that shows the many different ways we are "on the go." In advance, cover a large bulletin board or wall area with white butcher paper to serve as the background. Sketch the background into three sections to represent the land, sea, and sky. Make sponge paintbrushes by clipping clothespins to sponge squares. Provide a variety of craft supplies, including paint; cotton; construction paper; tissue paper; pipe cleaners; and magazine pictures of cars, bikes, trucks, trains, boats, and planes. Have students use the following suggestions to make the display:

- Use the sponge paintbrushes to dab blue paint at the bottom of the mural to make the sea. Use light-blue paint at the top for the sky. Create a 3-D sky by adding stretched-out cotton to the sky before the paint dries.

- Make the land by gluing on small pieces of torn green construction paper and tissue paper.

- Use black pipe cleaners to create the streets and railroad tracks.

- Use fabric scraps and felt to make the landscape.

- Glue transportation magazine pictures to the appropriate places on the mural.

- Title the mural *On the Go with Room ____*.

Charts

Make a chart titled *Terrific Transportation Words* to post in the classroom. Ask students to list words that relate to transportation. Throughout the unit, invite students to record on the chart theme-related vocabulary words they have learned. To further challenge students, have them classify the new words as nouns, adjectives, verbs, and adverbs, or put them under specific categories such as *Land Transportation, Water Transportation,* and *Air Transportation.* For extra fun, write the words on paper-vehicle cutouts and include them as part of the class mural (see page 4).

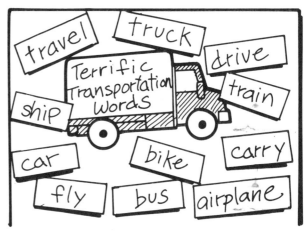

Also make a KWL chart that includes the column headers *What We **K**now about Transportation, What We **W**ant to Learn about Transportation,* and *What We **L**earned about Transportation.* At the beginning of the unit, have students brainstorm ideas for the first two columns. At the end of the unit, invite students to share what they learned about transportation as you record their ideas on the chart. Invite students to review and compare what they knew about transportation to what they learned.

"Things That Go" Wind Sock

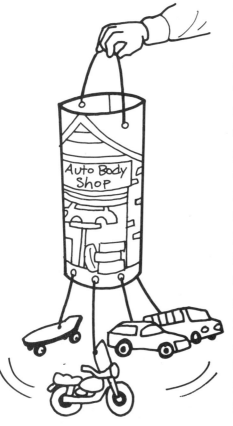

Invite the class to make "Things That Go" wind socks to hang in the classroom. Give each student a photocopy of the Things That Go sheet (page 6) and the Auto Body Shop sheet (page 7). Have students color and cut out the auto body shop and vehicles. Give each student an 11" x 17" (28 cm x 43 cm) piece of construction paper. Have students place the construction paper horizontally on their desk. Ask students to glue their auto body shop to the middle of the construction paper. Have them twist the paper into the shape of a cylinder and glue or staple the edges (as shown). Have students hole-punch eight holes evenly spaced along the bottom of the cylinder. Invite students to glue each vehicle to the end of a piece of yarn, thread each piece through a hole, and tie it off. Extend learning by asking students to write the name of each vehicle on the back of the corresponding picture. Ask students to hole-punch two holes on opposite sides at the top of the wind sock. Have students thread yarn through the holes to create a hanger so the wind socks may be displayed in the doorways and windows of the classroom.

Things That Go

Transportation © 1999 Creative Teaching Press

Management

The amount of time you spend on this unit depends upon your goals and objectives. As you teach students about transportation, consider the following suggestions:

- Vary instructional strategies so activities validate different learning modalities—auditory, visual, tactile, and kinesthetic. Encourage students to investigate, analyze, speculate about, and verify answers to problems. Follow up verbal instructions with visual cues and hands-on applications.

- Encourage peer interaction. Organize your class into small groups so students can share creative ideas, art supplies, and manipulatives. Use the reproducible certificates (page 31) to recognize and reward your "transportation experts."

- Provide learning centers with multilevel, self-paced activities addressing various learning styles. Store learning-center materials in colorful, portable containers next to each corresponding station. Have students place completed paperwork in holding trays, file folders, or work cubbies. Post a laminated class list, and ask students to check off their name when they have completed an activity.

- Encourage family involvement through written correspondence (see the reproducible parent letter, page 10) and take-home activities. Provide books (see Recommended Books, page 32) that students can check out and share with family members.

◆ ◆ ◆ ◆ ◆ ◆ ◆ ◆ ◆ ◆ ◆ ◆ ◆

Assessment

Assessment should be an integrated part of regular instruction. Include a variety of approaches, such as scoring rubrics (see Performance Evaluation, page 9), anecdotal records, and student portfolios. Encourage children to share in the evaluation of their work, selecting and self-evaluating completed assignments to include in their portfolios. (Date all portfolio entries so they can be chronologically compared at any time.) Conduct individual student conferences to verify understanding of concepts as well as to assess the ability to follow directions. Ask students to discuss their most interesting activity, prompting them with questions such as *What did you learn by doing this activity?* or *What might you do differently if you tried this activity again?*

Performance Evaluation

Student _____   Date _____

Check the level that best reflects the student's performance.

Activity:	Performance Level			
_____	Excellent	Very Good	Good	Needs Improvement
Shows motivation and curiosity for learning.				
Demonstrates full understanding of concepts.				
Clearly communicates and listens to others.				
Accurately records and describes observations.				
Uses knowledge to solve problems or extend thinking.				
Comments:				

Rubric

Excellent
Goes beyond competency, adding creativity and insight to overall performance. Shows initiative and takes charge of own learning. Listens attentively to others. Shows advanced critical thinking skills. Written work is polished, with detailed explanations that extend into other subject areas.

Very Good
Uses skills effectively. Listens well during discussions, contributing thoughtful ideas and opinions. Work is neat and accurate, showing evidence of higher-level thinking. Does not take risks or extend ideas into other subject areas.

Good
Shows much effort and desire to learn but is still working on mastery of skills. Written work is accurate but shows little creativity or higher-level thinking. Follows directions well but needs extra encouragement and time to organize work.

Needs Improvement
Lacks organization and effort. Student is unsure of how to use materials or uses them incorrectly. Written work is inaccurate and shows little or no creativity. Does not follow directions and needs additional guidance to perform general tasks.

...y unit on
...ading, writing,
...ussing topics such as
... transportation, types of trans-
..., and how transportation is used.

To help us with our "transportation studies,"
we would appreciate you sending any of the
following materials to class with your child:

aluminum foil	*buttons*	*empty quart-size milk or juice cartons*
clothespins	*cotton balls*	*colored tissue paper*
empty matchboxes	*craft sticks*	*Styrofoam meat trays*
felt and fabric scraps	*pipe cleaners*	*small and large paper plates*
frosting can lids	*sponges*	*frozen juice can lids*
old magazines	*string*	*ring reinforcements*
toilet-paper tubes	*yarn*	

Share in your child's excitement for learning by completing the following activities together:

- ◆ Set aside time each night to read aloud books about transportation, such as *Frank and Ernest: On the Road* by Alexandra Day and *Mr. Gumpy's Motor Car* by John Burningham. Be sure to include a variety of stories, including folktales, adventures, and mysteries.

- ◆ Visit an automotive, flight, train, or space museum to learn more about transportation. Take pictures while at the museum, and use the pictures to make a transportation photo album that includes facts about each method of transportation.

- ◆ Take your child on a "mystery" walking trip. Find a simple map, or draw a map of your neighborhood. Mark the route you want your child to follow. Help your child follow the route on the map to reach the mystery destination. During the walking trip, ask your child to point out or draw the various types of transportation he or she sees. The mystery destination could be the library where your child reads or hears a story about transportation, or it could be a neighborhood park.

Thank you for your support.

Sincerely,

Transportation © 1999 Creative Teaching Press

Reading & Language Arts

Peek-a-Boo Plane

Read aloud stories about airplanes, such as *Planes* by Anne Rockwell or *Flying* by Gail Gibbons. Discuss the types of planes seen in the story as well as the actions made by the planes. Explain that words describing actions are called *verbs*. Brainstorm with students a list of other types of transportation and the actions they perform (e.g., ships–sail, trains–carry, mail trucks–deliver). Distribute a photocopy of the Peek-a-Boo Plane sheet (page 12) and a 2"-wide (5 cm-wide) sentence strip to each student. Have

students cut out both paper airplanes and the middle window in each picture and align both airplanes so that the middle windows are even. Invite students to staple or glue the airplanes together at each end so they become one, leaving the top and bottom of the airplane left unstapled. Have students hold their sentence strip vertically and write on one side the names of various types of transportation. Ask students to write on the opposite side the related verb right behind the mode of transportation. Then ask students to slip the sentence strip in between the two airplanes so that the name of a mode of transportation appears in the window. Have students read each word and flip the airplane over to see the matching verb. For extra fun, invite students to act out the action of each type of vehicle.

◆ ◆ ◆ ◆ ◆ ◆ ◆ ◆ ◆ ◆ ◆ ◆

Transportation Poetry

Teach students the following train poem and corresponding finger movements:

The Train

Here is the train.	(make a fist with right hand)
Here is the track.	(hold left arm level)
The train goes forward.	
Now it comes back.	(put fist on arm; move forward and back)
Here are the wheels	
Going clickety-clack.	(rotate hands around each other)
Poof! Goes the smoke,	
From the big smokestack!	(move hands up quickly over head)

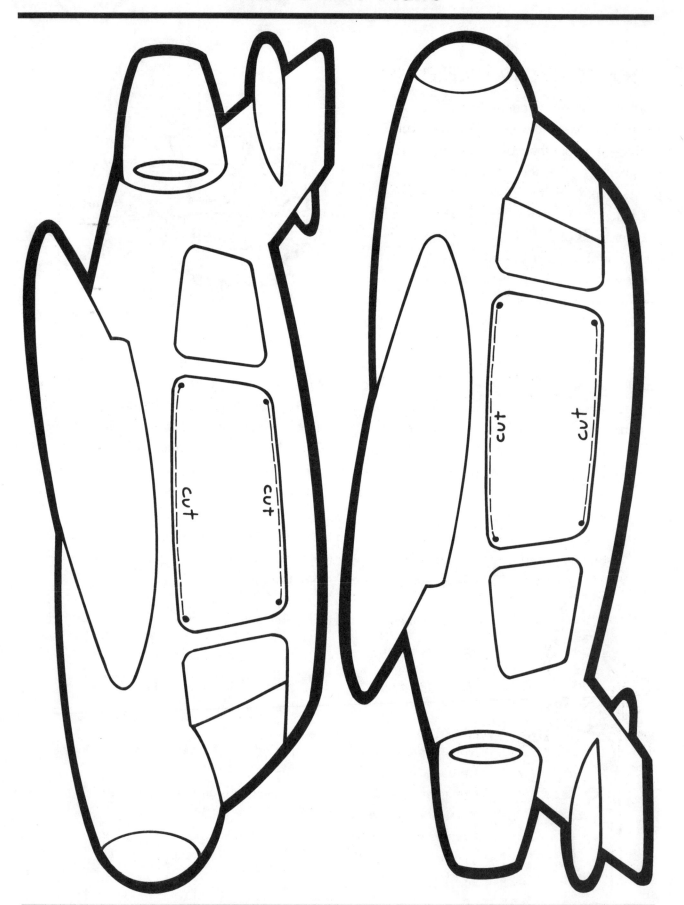

Journeys through Writing

Reproduce the bus-pattern sheet (page 14) for students to write on as they complete the following activities. (For some of these activities, you may choose to add writing lines to the page before photocopying it for students.)

- Invite each student to cut out the bus pattern and create a "magic bus." Students may decorate the magic bus with a variety of collage materials, including glitter, buttons, sequins, stickers, pasta, and yarn. Extend the fun by asking students to write "magic bus stories" on an additional bus-pattern sheet with lines. Have students write about their magic bus and why it is magical. Encourage students to share their decorated bus and magic bus story with classmates. Display the magic buses and stories on a bulletin board.

- Read aloud and discuss *On the Go* by Rozanne Lanczak Williams (Creative Teaching Press). Ask students *How are you on the go?* and *What kinds of transportation do you use to get from place to place?* For extra fun, create a class book called *We Are on the Go!* Have students bring from home a photo of themselves and their family on the go. The photo may include family cars, motorcycles, recreational vehicles (e.g., mountain bikes, wave runners, boats), or any other interesting vehicles they see while on an outing or family trip. Ask students to glue the photo onto the bus-pattern sheet and write a brief description next to it.

- Read aloud *Barney Bear, World Traveler* by Trisha Callella et al. (Creative Teaching Press). Discuss the various types of transportation Barney Bear used in his world travels. Also, call students' attention to the use of prepositions in the story. Ask the class to think about a trip they took with their family. Ask questions such as *Where did you go on your vacation?* and *What kinds of transportation were used during the trip?* Have each student make a postcard for a friend or relative out of the bus-pattern sheet. Students can draw a picture of a place they visited and write about it.

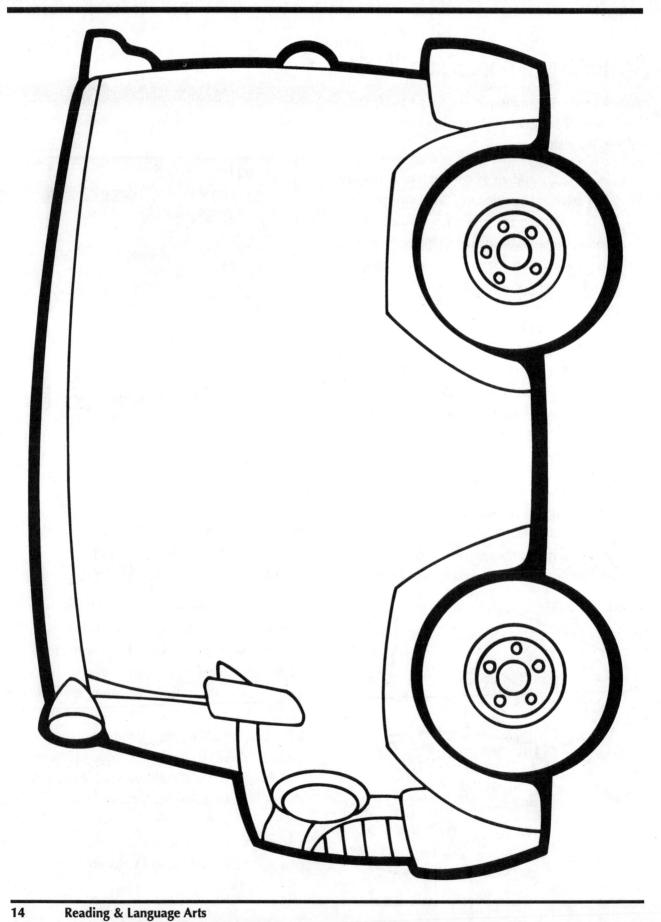

Mathematics

All Aboard the Number Train

Read aloud stories about trains, such as *Freight Train* by Donald Crews or *The Train* by David McPhail. Extend learning by having each student build a number train. In advance, collect recycled milk or juice cartons from the cafeteria and cut off the tops. Give each student four cartons. Provide the students with craft supplies, such as craft sticks, fabric, yarn, crayons, glitter, scissors, and glue. Have students use the following directions to make their number train:

1. Color and cut out the Number Train patterns (pages 16 and 17).

2. Number the train-car pieces, and glue one car to each carton.

3. Use craft sticks and various craft items to make passengers.

4. Hole-punch two holes on opposite sides of each train car (carton). String yarn through the holes to connect the train cars.

5. Fill each train car with the number of craft stick passengers that corresponds to the number on the train car.

To further challenge students, ask them to write addition, subtraction, or multiplication facts on the passenger sticks. Encourage students to place the number of passengers in the train car that corresponds to the correct answer.

Number Train

Number Train

Ordinal Numbers

Explain to students that ordinal numbers are used to mark a place or give the order of directions. Distribute a photocopy of the Who Came in First? sheet (page 19) to each student. Ask students to color the race cars, cut them out, and glue them in the correct ordinal number order. For extra fun, give students ink pads to share (use washable ink pads), and invite them to follow these steps for making a fingerprint "train":

- First, using one hand, press each finger, beginning with the thumb and following with each succeeding finger, onto an ink pad.

- Second, press each stamped finger, beginning with the thumb, horizontally onto a piece of paper so that the fingerprints make a straight line.

- Third, use a pencil or dark marker to make the wheels. Draw two sets of small circles on the bottom of each fingerprint, except for the thumbprint (engine).

- Fourth, draw one large circle, two small circles, and a triangle on the bottom of the engine (as shown).

- Fifth, draw a circular headlight and a rectangular-shaped smokestack on the engine. Draw smoke coming out of the smokestack.

- Sixth, use a pencil or dark marker to draw windows on each fingerprint, except for the engine. Draw black dots inside the windows to make passengers.

- Seventh, draw a rectangle at the back of the engine to make a door. Draw a black dot inside the rectangle for the door handle.

In advance, make a thumbprint train for students' reference.

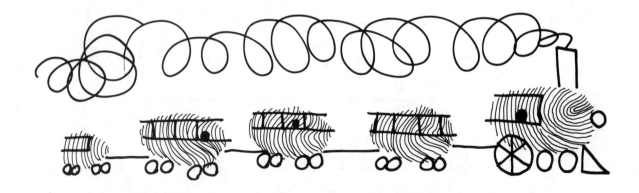

Who Came in First?

Eighth 8th

Second 2nd

Fifth 5th

Ninth 9th

Third 3rd

Sixth 6th

First 1st

Fourth 4th

Seventh 7th

Directions: Color and cut out the race cars. Glue the cars into the boxes on the track to show who came in first through ninth place in the car race.

Science

Transportation Study

Discuss with students the meaning of transportation. Teach students that transportation is the act of moving people or goods from one place to another. Provide the class with pictures of vehicles from magazines or books. Encourage students to notice that different types of transportation move in various ways. Vehicles move by driving (e.g., cars, trucks, trains), flying (e.g., airplanes, helicopters), or sailing (e.g., boats, ships). Invite students to experience how vehicles move goods from one place to another by completing the following activity.

Brainstorm with students the ways a pile of wooden blocks can be moved from one end of the classroom to the other. (A pile of any kind of object may be used.) Ask students to predict how many trips it will take to move the blocks using each method. Create a "Let's Move It" chart that lists methods of transportation and predictions of how many trips it will take to move the blocks. Invite small groups of students to test their methods of transportation, and record the results on the chart. Have students compare their predictions with their final results.

How ?	Predicted Number of Trips	Actual Trips Taken
Carrying by Hand	9	20
Pushing a Box		
Pulling a Wagon		
Moving a Toy Dump Truck		

Let's Move It !

◆ ◆ ◆ ◆ ◆ ◆ ◆ ◆ ◆ ◆ ◆ ◆ ◆ ◆

Will It Float like a Boat?

Prepare a chart that has a *Floats like a Boat* column and a *Sinks* column. Ask the class why they think boats can float. Divide the class into groups of three to four students. Provide each group with different kinds of items, such as marbles, apples, paper clips,

craft sticks, balls of clay, sponges, erasers, pencils, and pennies. (Any kind of small waterproof item may be used.) Ask the groups to discuss predictions about whether their items will float like a boat or sink in a bowl or tub filled with water. After the groups make their predictions, invite them to float the items in a tub of water. Encourage the groups to record their results on the class chart by drawing a picture of each item in the column that corresponds to their findings.

Gravity and Transportation

Discuss with students the influence of gravity on transportation. Explain that gravity is the force that pulls things to the earth or ground. Brainstorm the types of transportation that move on the ground and the types that are able to fly and resist gravity. Provide students with a variety of toy cars and trucks, and invite them to see how gravity influences their movement by having them experiment with the following activities:

- Push the toy cars or trucks and see how far they will travel.

- Build a ramp by leaning a book against a brick, a piece of wood, or a thick book. Place a toy car or truck at the top of the ramp and see how far it will travel once it gets down the ramp. Try various inclines of the ramp by adding bricks, wood, or books to make it steeper.

- Have students work in groups to build their own ramp out of a variety of materials (e.g., blocks, cardboard, construction paper, paper-towel tubes, toilet-paper tubes, scissors, milk cartons, tape, and cereal or tissue boxes). Ask them to build a ramp that will make their car or truck travel the farthest. Encourage the groups to share their "ramp creations."

Social Studies & Geography

Map Skills

Read aloud books about maps, such as *Maps* by Joellyn Thrall Cicciarelli (Creative Teaching Press). Discuss with students how maps are tools used to help with direction. There are many kinds of maps that assist people with travel. Road maps help people locate streets and highways. Railroad maps show the major train routes to help direct conductors as well as passengers. Pilots and passengers use maps with airline routes to check mileage as well as direction of travel.

Divide the class into small groups, and provide them with a road map, a railroad map, or a United States map. Encourage students to locate general landmarks such as cities, states, and highways. Then ask them to find specific streets, the shortest route to a destination, their house, and their school.

◆ ◆ ◆ ◆ ◆ ◆ ◆ ◆ ◆ ◆ ◆ ◆ ◆ ◆

Staying Safe with Seat Belts

Read aloud *Safety Counts!* by Joel Kupperstein (Creative Teaching Press). Discuss the importance of seat belts. Ask students when they should wear a seat belt and why it is important. Encourage students to write and illustrate their own short story about safety titled *Staying Safe with Seat Belts*. Bind their stories into a class book.

◆ ◆ ◆ ◆ ◆ ◆ ◆ ◆ ◆ ◆ ◆ ◆ ◆ ◆

Community-Helper Vehicles

Read aloud stories about community helpers (see Recommended Books, page 32). Discuss the specific kinds of transportation people use to do their job to help the community. Invite students to complete the Community-Helper Vehicles sheet (page 23).

Name _____ Date _____

Community-Helper Vehicles

Directions: Color the vehicles and the community helpers. Draw a line to match each vehicle to the correct community helper.

Music & Drama

Little Airplane

I'm a little airplane
Above the clouds I go.
Banking right, banking left
Flying high and low.
Now it's time for me to land
I see the airport runway.
Gently, gently I touch down.
I'll take you with me some day.

—Rozanne Lanczak Williams

Flying High

Give each student a copy of the Pilot's Hat sheet (page 25) to color, cut apart, assemble, and wear. Invite students to pretend they are pilots and "fly" a little airplane as they recite the poem.

♦ ♦ ♦ ♦ ♦ ♦ ♦ ♦ ♦ ♦ ♦ ♦ ♦

Favorite Transportation Songs

Invite the class to sing popular songs about transportation, such as "Row, Row, Row Your Boat." Invite students to pretend they are in a small boat with a friend. Have students sit with a partner on the floor with their knees bent and feet together. Ask them to hold hands and gently pull each other back and forth, as if they are rowing. Teach students the revised verses to the tune of "Row, Row, Row Your Boat."

For extra fun, invite groups to sing the different verses. Encourage them to dramatize their verse while standing in front of the On the Go wall mural (see page 4).

Extend learning by singing other popular songs about trains, such as "I've Been Workin' on the Railroad," "She'll Be Comin' Round the Mountain," and "Down By the Station." Read aloud *Wheels On The Bus* by Raffi, and teach students the song to go along with the book.

Fly, fly, fly your plane
Way up in the sky.
Merrily, merrily, merrily, merrily,
It's so fun to fly.

Drive, drive, drive your car,
Up and down the street.
Merrily, merrily, merrily, merrily,
Isn't driving neat?

Sail, sail, sail your boat,
On the ocean blue.
Merrily, merrily, merrily, merrily,
I'm the captain, you're the crew.

Pilot's Hat

Directions: Color and cut out the pilot's hat. Staple a strip of construction paper around the back of the cap to make a headband.

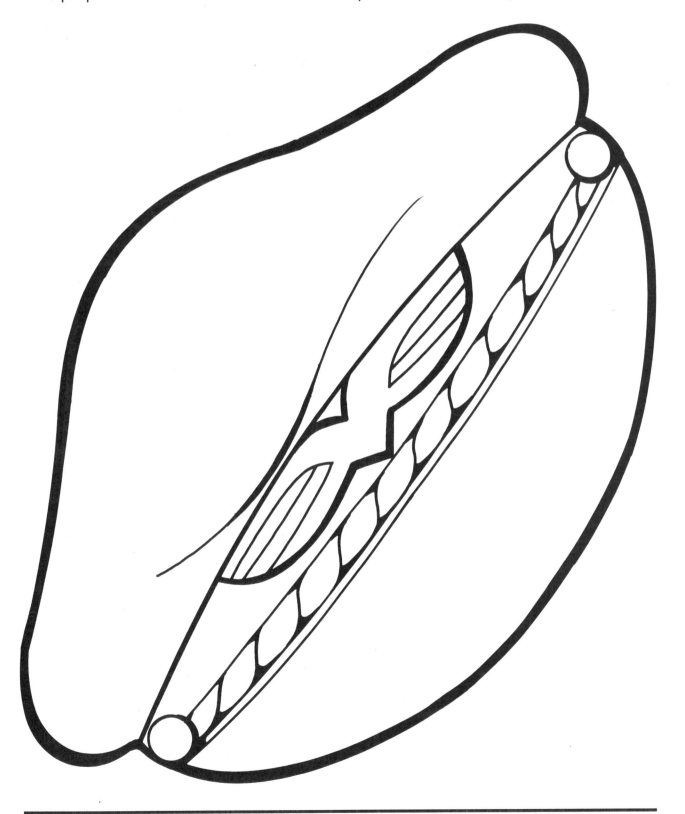

Physical Education

Safari Tour

Invite the class to go on an imaginary safari tour. Take students to a large playfield, and have them stand in one long line with an arm's length between them. Lead the class through the safari. Demonstrate the following movements to help them develop flexibility, strength, coordination, and endurance:

1. Fly to a faraway destination: *arms up, swaying to the left and to the right.*
2. Land the plane and unload your supplies: *stretch arms way up high, and then down low (do this many times).*
3. Drive your jeep into the deep, dark jungle: *hold onto steering wheel, change gears.*
4. Walk into jungle: *lift knees high when taking steps.*
5. Hurry, get away from the lion!: *climb tree with arms.*
6. Row your boat down a river: *hold oar and paddle.*
7. Oops! You fall in the river. Swim quickly before the crocodiles eat you: *swim freestyle with arms.*
8. Run away from a herd of elephants: *run in place.*
9. Cross a rope bridge: *move feet heel to toe with arms outstretched.*
10. Arrive back at the airport and fly home: *arms up like wings.*

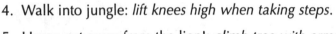

Train Relay Game

Take students to a large playfield. Set up four cones spaced apart at the end of the field. Divide the class into four teams, and have each group line up single file, with their hands placed on the shoulders of the person in front of them, to form a "train" (the first person is the "conductor"). At the signal (e.g., a whistle blow, or shout *All aboard*), each team hops to the cone, around the cone, and back to the "station." Each student must perform the actions without letting go of the person in front of him or her. Continue to play until each team member has had a chance to be the conductor. The team that returns to the station first the most times is the overall winner of the relay game.

Arts & Crafts

Constructing Crazy Cars

Ask students to bring two frozen juice can lids or frosting can lids from home. Tell students the lids will be used as "wheels" for "crazy" cars. Provide each child with a piece of construction paper, crayons, aluminum foil, glitter, and glue. Ask each student to glue their lids to the bottom of the construction paper and design a crazy car around the two wheels using the craft items. (Any kind of vehicle with two wheels may be created.) Encourage students to draw a background to go along with their vehicle. For extra fun, have students share their crazy car with the class. Display the students' creations on a bulletin board.

◆ ◆ ◆ ◆ ◆ ◆ ◆ ◆ ◆ ◆ ◆ ◆ ◆

Safety Signs

In advance, cut out of tagboard various shapes such as circles, octagons, pentagons, and diamonds. Review the shapes with the class. Explain that the number of sides relates to the name of the shape. Ask students if they can think of any signs that are these shapes. Divide the class into groups and provide one stencil of each shape to each group. Distribute various craft supplies (e.g., red and yellow construction paper, black crayons or markers, and craft sticks), and have students follow the directions below to make safety signs for students to use and enjoy.

1. Trace one yellow circle, one yellow diamond, one yellow pentagon, and one red octagon.

2. On the yellow circle, draw a railroad crossing symbol.

3. On the yellow diamond, draw a bicycle.

4. On the yellow pentagon, draw an adult and a child crossing the street and carrying books.

5. Write STOP in capital letters on the red octagon.

6. Cut out the shapes, and glue a craft stick to the back of each sign.

7. Review the uses of each safety sign.

Milk-Carton Steamships

Invite students to become "ship builders" and create milk-carton "steamships." First, have them cover an empty quart-size milk carton with aluminum foil. Next, have them lay the carton on its side and glue empty matchboxes (or other small boxes) to the top of the "ship." Then, have students cut toilet-paper tubes and paper-towel tubes into different sizes. Ask students to glue or tape the tubes onto the top of the small boxes to make "smokestacks." Add cotton balls to the top of the tubes for "steam." Finally, invite students to glue buttons or ring reinforcements to the sides of the steamship for "portholes."

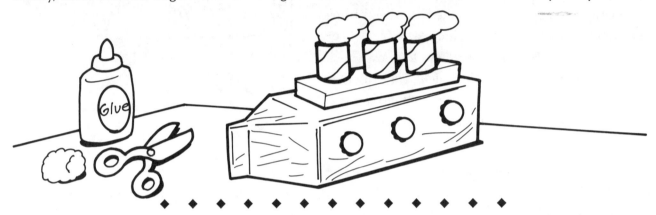

Cool Cardboard Cars

Use various craft materials (e.g., large cardboard boxes, small and large paper plates, Styrofoam meat trays, large brads, heavy string or yarn, paint and paintbrushes, scissors) to create a cool cardboard "car" for each student to enjoy.

1. Cut a hole in the bottom of a large cardboard box. The hole must be large enough so that a child can fit through it. Cut off flaps.

2. Paint the box, and let it dry.

3. Poke two holes on the front of the box, and attach two small paper plates with brads for "headlights."

4. Attach two large paper plates with brads to each side of the box to make the "wheels."

5. Write a student's name on a Styrofoam meat tray for a "license plate," and glue it to the front of the box.

6. Poke two holes in the top of the box, and attach yarn so the car can be worn around a student's neck.

7. Invite students to participate in a "car parade" where they walk around the classroom displaying their cars.

Banana Boats

Supplies:
- 2 small cans pineapple chunks
- can opener
- mixing bowl
- 4 large bananas
- plastic knives
- paper plates
- peanut butter
- raisins
- 20 seedless grapes
- toothpicks

Invite students to make "banana boats" to share and enjoy. Drain the pineapple juice and set it aside in a mixing bowl. Ask students to peel the bananas. Divide the bananas in half by slicing vertically down the middle. Coat the bananas in the pineapple juice. Give each student half of a banana on a paper plate. Ask students to spread peanut butter across their banana. Have them add "crew members" by attaching raisins to the peanut butter. Encourage students to make "masts" and "sails" by poking grapes and pineapple chunks through toothpicks. Have students stick the toothpicks into their banana. (Note: Carefully supervise children when they use sharp objects such as toothpicks.) For extra fun, encourage students to create names and stories for their banana boat. (serves 8)

◆ ◆ ◆ ◆ ◆ ◆ ◆ ◆ ◆ ◆ ◆ ◆ ◆

Celery Carts

Supplies:
- peanut butter or cream cheese
- celery stalks cut into small pieces
- plastic knives
- toothpick halves
- peeled carrots sliced into circles for wheels
- raisins

Ask children to spread peanut butter or cream cheese onto celery pieces with plastic knives. Have them attach the "wheels" by poking the toothpick halves through the bottom of carrot slices and into the celery. The children may add the "passenger" raisins to the top of the celery "cart." (serves 10)

 # Special Events

Field Trips

There are many places where students may learn more about transportation. Take the class to a train, car, flight, or space museum. Set up a tour of a harbor or a ship. Arrange for a visit to the airport or train station. For extra fun, take the class on a "walking field trip" to a local fire station, a gas station, a car dealership, or an automobile assembly plant. Take pictures of the trip, and record all the fun in a class big book titled *The Travels of Room ___*.

♦ ♦ ♦ ♦ ♦ ♦ ♦ ♦ ♦ ♦ ♦ ♦ ♦ ♦

Transportation Experts

Invite specialists such as pilots, conductors, air-traffic controllers, coastguardsman, ship captains, bus drivers, and police officers to speak to your class. Have students prepare a list of questions to ask guest speakers. Be sure to take pictures of these special events to add to the class scrapbook or post as a part of a bulletin-board display.

Choo, Choo! Good for You!

_____
(name)

is on the right track in _____
(subject)

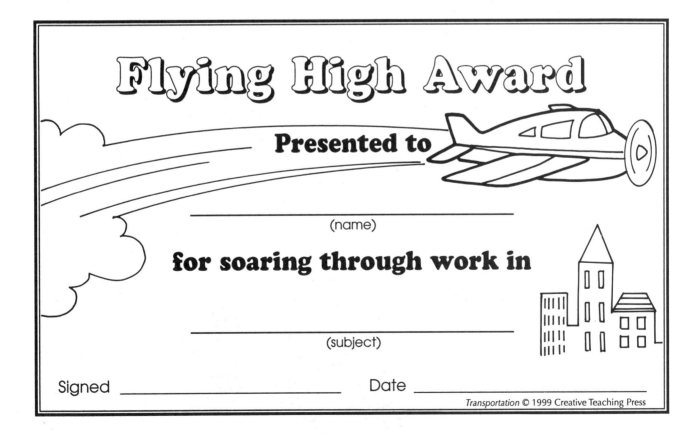

Signed _____ Date _____

Transportation © 1999 Creative Teaching Press

Flying High Award

Presented to

_____
(name)

for soaring through work in

_____
(subject)

Signed _____ Date _____

Transportation © 1999 Creative Teaching Press

# Recommended Books

Airplanes by Bryon Barton

Barney Bear, World Traveler by Trisha Callella et al. (Creative Teaching Press)

Bicycle Race by Donald Crews

Big City Port by Betsy Maestro and Ellen Del Vecchio

Boats by Bryon Barton

Boats by Anne Rockwell

Cars by Anne Rockwell

Cars and How They Go by Joanna Cole

Cars and Trucks and Things That Go by Richard Scarry

Choo Choo by Virginia Lee Burton

Eye Openers: Diggers and Dump Trucks by Angela Royston

Farmers (Community Helpers Series) by Dee Ready

Firefighters (Community Helpers Series) by Dee Ready

Flying by Gail Gibbons

Frank and Ernest: On the Road by Alexandra Day

Freight Train by Donald Crews

Garbage Collectors (Community Helpers) by Tami Deedrick

Harbor by Donald Crews

How Many Trucks Can A Tow Truck Tow? by Charlotte Pomerantz

Just Graph It! by Sandi Hill (Creative Teaching Press)

The Little Engine that Could by Watty Piper

Maps by Joellyn Thrall Cicciarelli (Creative Teaching Press)

Morningtown Ride by Malvina Reynolds

Mr. Gumpy's Motor Car by John Burningham

On the Go by Rozanne Lanczak Williams (Creative Teaching Press)

Pigs Ahoy! by David McPhail

Planes by Anne Rockwell

Police Officers (Community Helpers Series) by Dee Ready

Row, Row, Row Your Boat by Pippa Goodhart

Safety Counts! by Joel Kupperstein (Creative Teaching Press)

School Bus by Donald Crews

She'll Be Coming Around the Mountain (Bank Street Ready-To-Read) by Emily Coplon

TRAIN (Eyewitness Books) by John Coiley

The Train by David McPhail

Trains by Bryon Barton

Transportation: Boats and Planes and Traveling Trains by Kim M. Thompson

Trucks by Bryon Barton

Up in the Air by Myra Cohn Livingston

Wheels On The Bus (Raffi Songs to Read) by Raffi

Zoorimes: Poems About Things That Go by Sylvia Cassedy